Flyers
A·N·I·M·A·L·S

Wild Animals

Written and edited by
Moira Butterfield
and Nicola Wright

Designed by
Chris Leishman

Illustrated by
Rachael O'Neill

Contents

All kinds of animals 2
Out in the cold 4
Under the sun 6
Deep in the forest 8
In the rainforest 10
On safari 12
In the outback 14
Under the ocean 16
On the mountainside 18
About town 20
Animals in danger 22
Index 24

LONDON · NEW YORK · SYDNEY

All kinds of animals

Wild animals live all over the world. There are many different kinds.

Elephant

The mammal group includes the largest animals.

Clown fish

Fish live in rivers, seas and oceans.

Grasshopper

There are millions of insects.

Snakes are reptiles.

Reptiles live in warm places.

This book is to be returned on or before
the last date stamped below

23 MAR 1999

NORFOLK LIBRARY
AND INFORMATION SERVICE

 100% recycled paper.

Amphibians can live in water and on land.

Frogs are amphibian.

All birds have wings and feathers.

Flamingo

Animal meals

Some animals only eat plants. They are called **herbivores**.

Zebra

Some animals only eat other animals. They are called **carnivores**.

Leopard

Animals that eat both meat and plants are called **omnivores**.

Out in the cold

At the top and bottom of the Earth there are cold, icy places where only a few different kinds of animals live.

Polar bears can smell seals several kilometres away.

Caribou (also called reindeer) live in big herds.

Lemmings live in warm underground burrows.

Flyer Fun Fact

Arctic hares and foxes turn white in winter. This helps to hide them on the snow.

Arctic tern

The far north is called the Arctic. In the middle there is frozen sea. Animals live on the land around the sea.

Musk oxen have warm shaggy coats that keep them warm.

Seals have a layer of fat that keeps them warm.

Antarctic

At the far south of the Earth there is some land called the Antarctic.

Penguins live around Antarctic shores. They cannot fly but they can swim well.

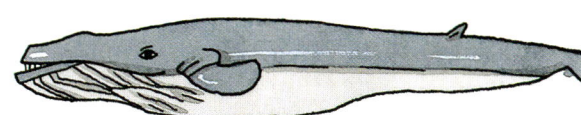

The world's biggest whale, the **blue whale**, swims in the Antarctic Ocean.

Deep in the forest

In northern parts of the world there are huge forests. Lots of different animals live amongst the trees.

Raccoon

Woodpeckers peck tree bark to find tasty insects.

Moose

Porcupines have strong claws for climbing trees. Their sharp quills protect them from attackers.

Brown bear

Owls nest in the trees. They hunt at night.

Squirrel

Beaver

A lynx is a type of wild cat.

Busy beavers

Beavers can gnaw through trees. They drag the branches to a stream to build a dam.

The dam creates a pond where the beavers store more branches.

In the winter the branches stay fresh in the icy pond, providing food for the beavers.

9

In the rainforest

Rainforests are hot, steamy places, where rain falls almost every day. The world's biggest rainforest grows around the Amazon River in South America. Here are some animals that live there.

Macaw (a kind of parrot)

Sloths spend their lives hanging from branches.

This colourful **morpho butterfly** measures 11cm across its wings.

These leaf-cutting **ants** are everywhere on the forest floor.

Howler monkeys get their name because they screech loudly.

Hummingbirds flap their wings between 50 and 80 times a second. This makes a loud humming noise.

The **anaconda** is the world's heaviest snake.

Getting around

Some monkeys have tails that they can curl round branches and use to grip on tightly.

Tree frogs have sticky pads on their toes for climbing trees.

Koala bears live in eucalyptus trees. They eat the leaves.

The **wombat** burrows amongst trees and rocks looking for plants to eat.

Pouch baby

A newborn kangaroo is only about 2.5cm long. It lives inside its mother's pouch until it is big enough to leave.

A baby kangaroo is called a **joey**.

Animals with pouches for their babies are called **marsupials**.

A **jellyfish** is kept afloat by a gas-filled bag.

Most **fish** swim in groups called shoals.

An **octopus** can change the colour of its skin to match the background.

Deep down

At the bottom of the ocean it is very dark and cold. The few animals that live there are strange and fierce-looking.

Deepsea fish often have big gaping mouths and long fangs.

Some deepsea fish have spots of light on their skin to attract prey.

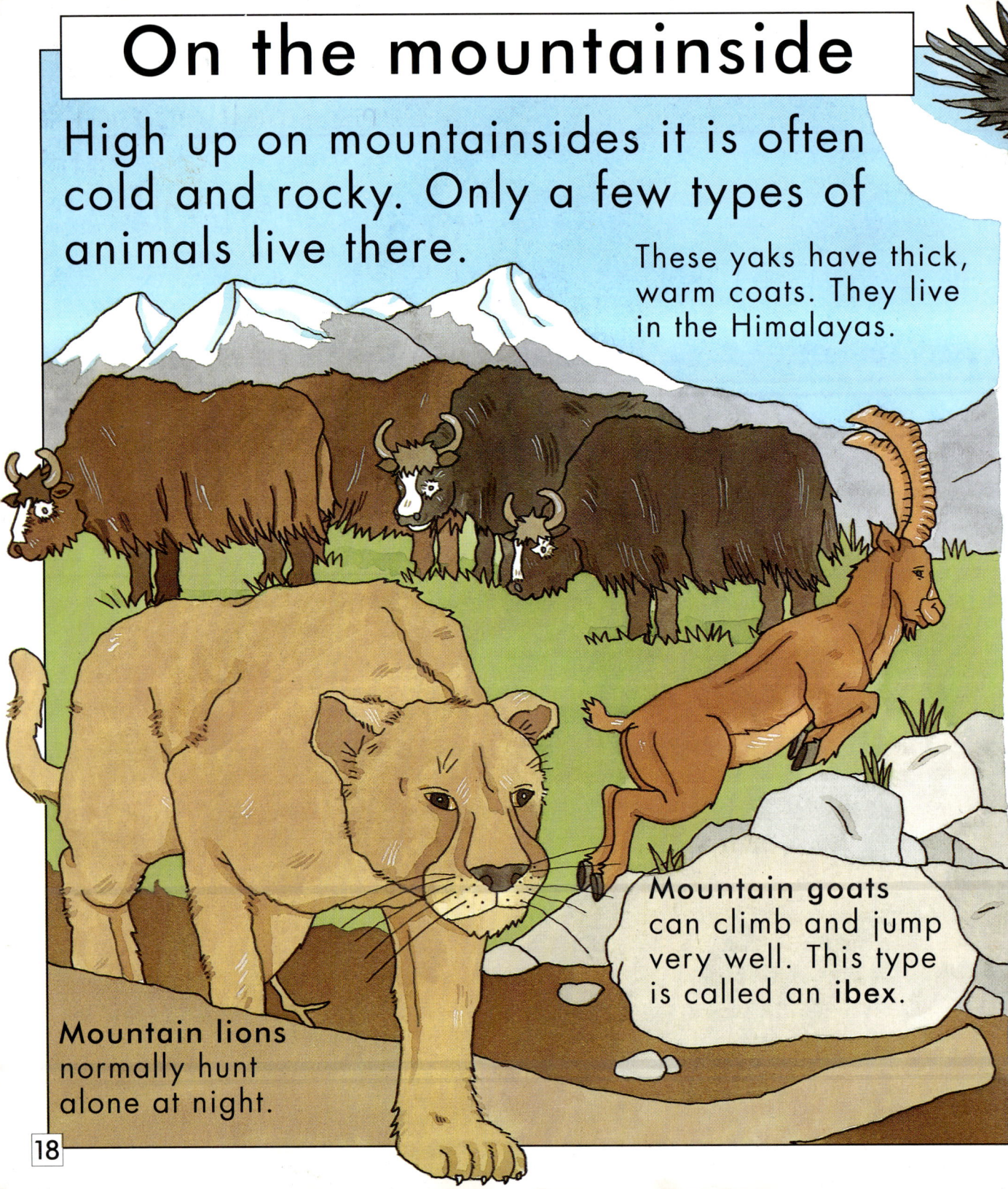

On the mountainside

High up on mountainsides it is often cold and rocky. Only a few types of animals live there.

These yaks have thick, warm coats. They live in the Himalayas.

Mountain goats can climb and jump very well. This type is called an **ibex**.

Mountain lions normally hunt alone at night.

Andean condor

Some mountain birds have large wings that are good for soaring on the wind.

Giant pandas are very shy and difficult to spot. They live in China.

Sleeping through

Some small mountain animals **hibernate**. They sleep through the cold winter.

Alpine marmots

They often sleep in cosy burrows underground.

When spring arrives they come outside to feed.

Flyer Fun Fact

In Florida, USA, alligators sometimes crawl into town!

Lizard (in warm countries)

Black rat

Insects, such as cockroaches

Mouse

Surprise visitors

Bears sometimes raid town dustbins in North America.

Elephants sometimes scavenge for food in parts of India.

Animals in danger

These animals are all endangered. This means that there are very few left in the world so they could become extinct.

Lemur (Madagascar)

Siberian tiger (Asia)

Green turtle (Pacific Ocean)

Humpback whale

Hyacinthine macaw (Amazon rainforest)

Mountain gorilla (Central Africa)

Snow leopard (Asia)

Animal threats

In some parts of the world **forests** are being cut down, destroying many animal homes.

Pollution can poison animals. **Litter** can harm them.

Some animals are **hunted** for their fur or their horns.

23

Index

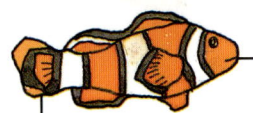

Alligator 21
Alpine marmot 19
Anaconda 11
Andean condor 19
Ants 10
Arctic fox 4
Arctic hare 4
Arctic tern 5
Baboon 13
Bat 20
Bear 8, 21
Beaver 9
Bird 20
Blue whale 5
Camel 7
Caribou 4
Cat 20
Cheetah 13
Clown fish 2
Cockroach 21
Duck-billed platypus 14
Elephant 2, 12, 21
Elf owl 6
Emu 14
Fish 2, 16, 17
Flamingo 3
Fox 4, 20
Frog 3, 11
Gazelle 12
Giant panda 19

Gila monster 7
Giraffe 13
Gorilla 23
Grasshopper 2
Green turtle 22
Hammerhead shark 16
Howler monkey 11
Hummingbird 11
Hyacinthine macaw 23
Hyena 13
Jellyfish 17
Kangaroo 14, 15
Kangaroo rat 6
Koala bear 15
Kookaburra 14
Lemming 4
Lemur 22
Leopard 3
Lion 12
Lizard 7, 21
Lynx 9
Macaw 10
Manta ray 16
Monkey 11
Moose 8
Morpho butterfly 10
Mountain goat 18
Mountain lion 18
Mouse 21
Musk oxen 5

Octopus 17
Owl 6, 9
Penguin 5
Polar bear 4
Porcupine 8
Raccoon 8
Rat 20
Rattlesnake 7
Rhinocerous 23
Roadrunner 6
Scorpion 6
Sea anemone 16
Sea cow 16
Sea cucumber 16
Seal 5
Sea snake 16
Siberian tiger 22
Sloth 10
Snake 2, 7
Snow leopard 23
Spadefoot toad 6
Squirrel 9
Star fish 16
Tree frog 11
Vulture 13
Wildebeest 12
Wombat 15
Woodpecker 8
Yak 18
Zebra 3, 12

This book was created by
Zigzag Publishing Ltd,
5 High Street, Cuckfield,
Sussex RH17 5EN

Series concept: Tony Potter
Design Manager: Kate Buxton
Production: Zoe Fawcett
Colour separations: ScanTrans, Singapore
Printed in Italy

First published in 1993 by Watts Books

Copyright © Zigzag Publishing Ltd

All rights reserved. No part of this publication may be reproduced, stored in a retrieval system or transmitted by any means, electronic, mechanical, photocopying or otherwise, without the prior permission of the publisher.

A CIP catalogue record for this book is available from the British Library.

Dewey Decimal Classification 591

ISBN 0 7496 1214 2

10 9 8 7 6 5 4 3 2 1

My Indian family history

Vic Parker

www.raintreepublishers.co.uk
Visit our website to find out more information about Raintree books.

To order:
☎ Phone 0845 6044371
📠 Fax +44 (0) 1865 312263
✉ Email myorders@raintreepublishers.co.uk

Customers from outside the UK please telephone +44 1865 312262

Raintree is an imprint of Capstone Global Library Limited, a company incorporated in England and Wales having its registered office at 7 Pilgrim Street, London, EC4V 6LB – Registered company number: 6695582

Text © Capstone Global Library Limited 2008
First published in paperback in 2009
The moral rights of the proprietor have been asserted.

All rights reserved. No part of this publication may be reproduced in any form or by any means (including photocopying or storing it in any medium by electronic means and whether or not transiently or incidentally to some other use of this publication) without the written permission of the copyright owner, except in accordance with the provisions of the Copyright, Designs and Patents Act 1988 or under the terms of a licence issued by the Copyright Licensing Agency, Saffron House, 6–10 Kirby Street, London EC1N 8TS (www.cla.co.uk). Applications for the copyright owner's written permission should be addressed to the publisher.

Editorial: Charlotte Guillain
Design: Joanna Hinton-Malivoire
Picture research: Erica Martin
Production: Duncan Gilbert
Illustrated by Jacqueline McQuade
Originated by Modern Age
Printed and bound in China by South China Printing Co. Ltd.

ISBN 978 0 4310 1507 1 (hardback)
ISBN 978 0 4310 1502 6 (paperback)

12 11
10 9 8 7 6 5 4 3 2

British Library Cataloguing in Publication Data
Parker, Vic
My Indian family history. - (Family histories)
305.9'06912
A full catalogue record for this book is available from the British Library.

Acknowledgements
The publishers would like to thank the following for permission to reproduce photographs:
© Alamy pp. **17** (Simon Reddy), **24**, **26** (Ian Shaw);
© Corbis pp. **11** (Bettmann), **21** (Reuters/Rupak De Chowdhuri); © Mary Evans Picture Library pp. **16**, **19**, **25**;
© Getty Images pp. **12** (Time Life Picture/Jack Birns), **20** (Hulton Archive); © Robert Harding Picture Library p. **9** (John Henry Claude Wilson); © popperfoto.com p. **15**

Cover photograph of girl reproduced with permission of © Punchstock (Uppercut RF).

Every effort has been made to contact copyright holders of any material reproduced in this book. Any omissions will be rectified in subsequent printings if notice is given to the publishers.

Disclaimer
All the Internet addresses (URLs) given in this book were valid at the time of going to press. However, due to the dynamic nature of the Internet, some addresses may have changed, or sites may have changed or ceased to exist since publication. While the author and publishers regret any inconvenience this may cause readers, no responsibility for any such changes can be accepted by either the author or publishers.

Contents

Savita's family history 4

Then and now 26

Savita's family tree 28

Finding out about your family history 29

More books to read 30

Websites 30

Glossary 31

Index 32

Words appearing in the text in bold, **like this**, are explained in the Glossary.

Savita's family history

My name is Savita. I am eight years old. I live with my mother, father, and older brother in a city called London.

London is England's **capital** city.

India is in South Asia, near Pakistan, China, Nepal, and Bangladesh.

My family comes from a country called India. India is one of the biggest countries in the world. It has hot deserts, steamy **rainforests**, and snowy mountains.

My family tree

My mother's parents

Bhupendra Patel (my grandfather) born 1926

Kamala Patel (my grandmother) born 1931

My father's parents

Govind Patel (my grandfather) born 1930

Deepika Patel (my grandmother) born 1933

Patel is a popular surname in Gujarat.

My grandparents grew up in India. One of my grandfathers, Bhupendra Patel, was born in a part of the country called Gujarat. Gujarat is by the sea. It is extremely dry and hot in summer.

My grandfather lived with his parents, three brothers, and two sisters in a small town.

My grandfather's town did not have electricity and people had to draw water from a well. My great-grandfather was a businessman. The family house was not very big. It had a kitchen, a living room, two bedrooms, and an outdoor toilet.

My great-grandmother could not read or write. But my great-grandfather thought school was very important. He made my grandfather work hard at lessons and do lots of extra study at home. My grandfather did not have much time to play.

At home my grandfather spoke a language called Gujarati. At school he also learned English.

This is the Hindu Temple of Somnath in Gujarat.

My grandfather and his family were **Hindus**, like many other people in India. They often went to a temple to pray. Every day, they prayed at a **shrine** in their home too.

It cost a lot of money for my grandfather to go to university.

When my grandfather was 16 years old, the family moved to a city called Rawalpindi. My grandfather went to university there and studied to be a doctor.

When my grandfather was 21 years old, Rawalpindi and other parts of India were made into a new country, Pakistan. Many people began fighting over who was going to live there. My grandfather and his family had to leave their home and get on a train to find safety.

My grandfather and his family became **refugees** with millions of other people.

My grandfather and his family went to one of India's busiest cities, Mumbai. They arrived with hardly any belongings or clothes. My grandfather and his brothers found work in a factory for very little money. The family had to live in a tin shack.

My grandfather and his family were very poor in Mumbai.

It was usual in those days for a **Hindu** bride and groom not to meet each other before their wedding.

My grandfather managed to finish his studies and become a doctor. When he was 32 years old, he married another doctor, called Kamala. Their families had arranged the marriage. My grandfather and Kamala met for the first time at their wedding.

My family tree

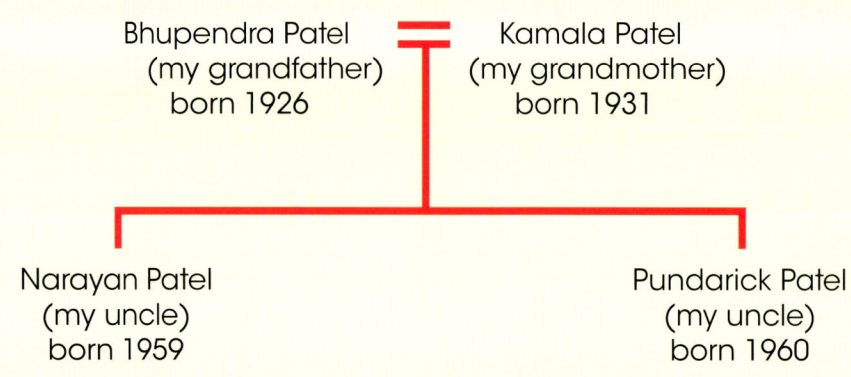

My grandmother moved in with my grandfather and his family. The couple soon had a baby boy. A year later, another baby boy was born. The growing family was very crowded and it was hard to make ends meet.

My grandmother's brother was living in Britain. He had gone there in 1947 to escape the fighting between people in India and Pakistan. Now he invited my grandfather to go and live in Britain with him. In 1961, my grandfather set off for England on a boat.

People took all their belongings from India to Britain.

My grandmother's brother lived in London. My grandfather stayed with him until he got a job as a doctor in a hospital. Then he rented a room on his own. Finding a room took a long time, because a lot of English people didn't want to rent a room to an Indian person.

More and more people from India were coming to live in Britain.

This is a *thali*, which is a typical Gujarati meal.

My grandfather found Britain cold and strange. When he spoke, people could not understand his **accent**. Meals in the hospital canteen were often made with meat. Like a lot of **Hindus**, my grandfather was **vegetarian**, so he couldn't eat this sort of food.

My family tree

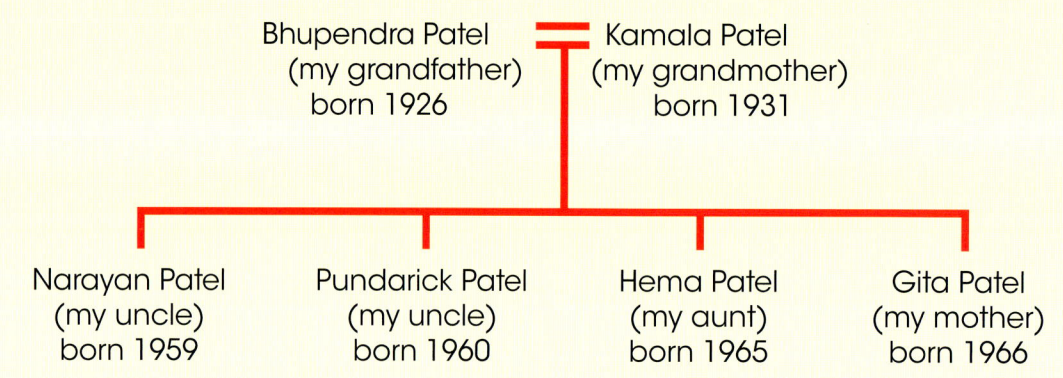

My grandfather saved money to bring my grandmother and their two sons to England. They rented a flat in a part of London called Harrow, where other Indian **Hindus** were living. They had two more children, both daughters.

At my mother's school, most of the children were white. Her best friend was a girl called Karen. Their favourite toys were Sindy dolls and space hoppers.

My mother was British, because she was born in Britain like her best friend, Karen.

Karen

My grandmother always wore a traditional Indian dress, called a sari. For special occasions, such as family celebrations and **Hindu** festivals, my mother wore a sari too. But she usually wore English clothes, like jeans and jumpers.

A sari is a long piece of cloth. You wrap one end around your waist to form a skirt. Then you drape the other end over your shoulders and head.

Diwali means "row of lights".

My mother's favourite Hindu festival was Diwali. People celebrate with coloured lights, candles, and fireworks. My mother enjoyed eating special sweets made from milk.

My mother and father had a big wedding party that lasted for three days.

My mother went to university and became a **chemist**. My grandparents introduced her to their friends' son. His name was Vijay and he was a **lawyer**. After a year getting to know each other, they got married.

My mother and father moved into their own house in Harrow. It was close to their parents' homes, so they could often all get together to share meals. Soon my mother and father had two children – my brother, Tushar, and then me!

My family tree

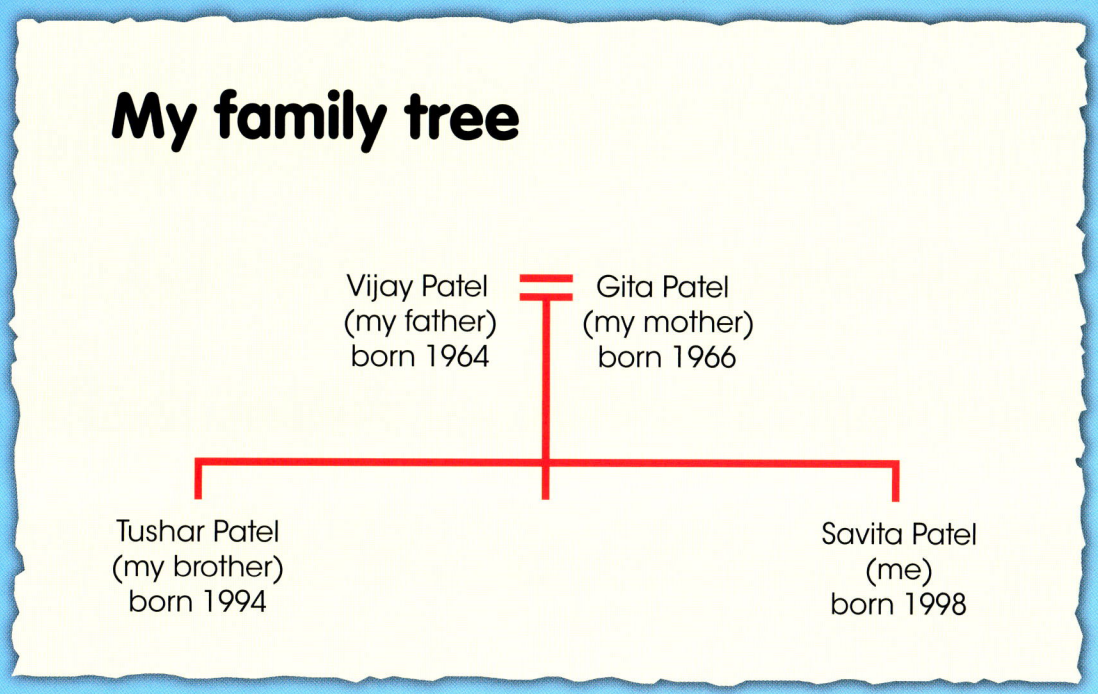

Vijay Patel
(my father)
born 1964

Gita Patel
(my mother)
born 1966

Tushar Patel
(my brother)
born 1994

Savita Patel
(me)
born 1998

I have grown up in Harrow. My friends at school have families from all over the world, including India. I would like to visit India one day.

I took this photograph of some of my school friends.

When I grow up I would like to dance and sing in an Indian film.

At school, my brother is studying an Indian instrument called the *tabla*. I am learning an Indian style of dancing called *kathak*. My school puts on a show every year and all my family comes to watch.

Then and now

My grandfather sat on the floor at school and leaned a few subjects, including English. At my school we learn about many things, including *kathak* dancing.

When my grandfather came to Britain, it was unusual to see people from India. Now there are families from India and many other countries living all over Britain.

Savita's family tree

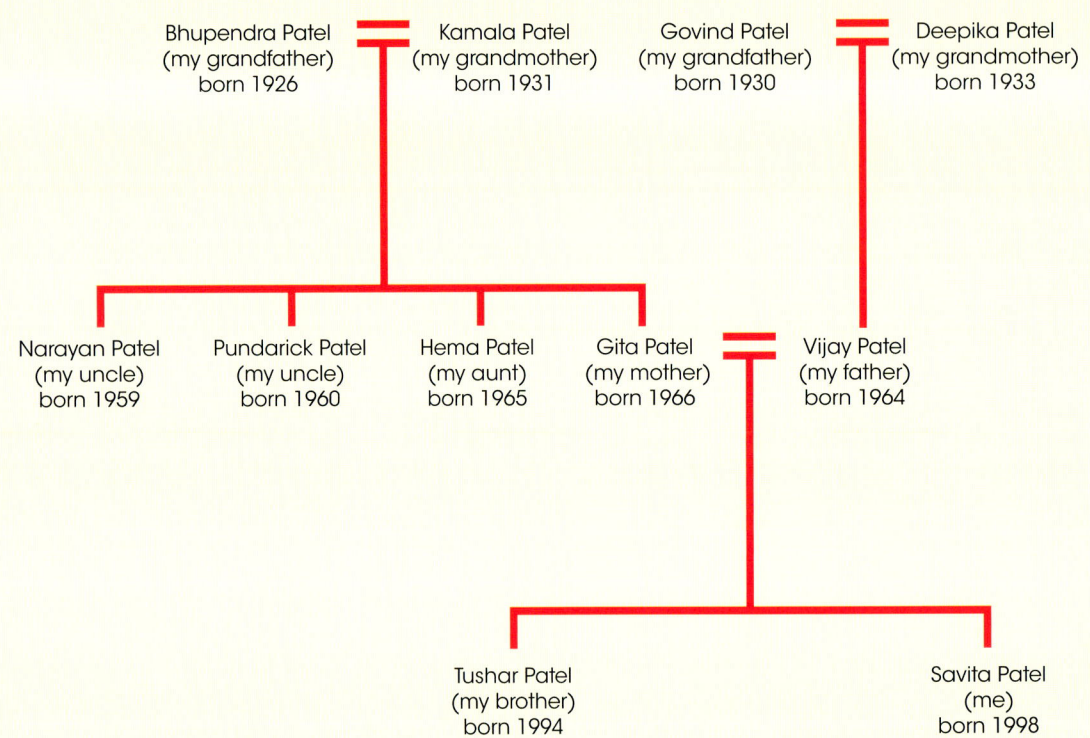

Finding out about your family history

- See if your family members have any photographs of when they got married, or when they were young. You could turn the photographs into a family history scrapbook. Get your family to write their memories next to the photographs.

- Ask your family about what life was like when they grew up. What toys did they like to play with? What food did they like to eat? What were their friends like? Did they go through difficult times? You could record them talking or write down what they tell you.

- Ask your mother, father, aunts, uncles and grandparents to help you make your own family tree.

- Look at a map and draw circles around the places where your family has lived. Find out about those places using books and websites. See if your family can take you on trips there.

More books to read

Celebrations: Divali, Denise Jordan (Raintree, 2003)

Prita Goes to India, Prodeepta Das (Frances Lincoln, 2005)

Traditional Tales from India, Victoria Parker (Belitha Press, 2001)

We're from India, Victoria Parker (Heinemann Library, 2005)

Websites

www.bbc.co.uk/history/walk/memory_index.shtml
This website gives you tips on finding out about your own family history.

http://pbskids.org/wayback/family/tree/index.html
This website helps you to put together your own family tree.

Glossary

accent way people from a certain area pronounce words

capital a country's capital city is its most important city

chemist person whose job is to prepare medicines

Hindu person who follows the Hindu religion

lawyer person whose job is to make sure people follow a country's laws

rainforest type of jungle found in hot, rainy places

refugee person who has had to leave their home and everything behind, because they are in danger

shrine special place set aside for people to go to pray – sometimes with a holy picture or statue in it

vegetarian if you are vegetarian, you do not eat meat

Index

accent 17

Bangladesh 5
Britain 15, 17

capital 4
China 5

Diwali 21
doctor 13, 16

family history 29, 30
family tree 6, 14, 18, 23, 28, 29, 30

Gujarat 6

Hindu 9, 13, 17, 18, 20, 21

India 5, 6, 11, 12, 15, 24

kathak 25

London 4, 16

Mumbai 12

Pakistan 5, 11, 15

rainforest 5
refugee 11

sari 20
school 8, 19

tabla 25
temple 9
thali 17
toys 19

university 10, 22

vegetarian 17

wedding 13, 22